A Tony Rouse Pocke

DARE 2 D.R.E.A.M.

The Basics of Building a Brand
(whether it be a person, product, or project...)

TONY ROUSE

DARE 2 D.R.E.A.M.

ISBN: 069267229X
ISBN-13: 978-0692672297

DEDICATION

This book is dedicated to the dreamers... Those individuals that never really quite fit in because they were always destined to stand out.

DARE 2 D.R.E.A.M.

CONTENTS

	Acknowledgments	i
	Introduction	1
STEP 1:	Define It.	5
STEP 2:	Design It.	7
STEP 3:	Rehearse It.	9
STEP 4:	Rewind It.	11
STEP 5:	Embrace It.	13
STEP 6:	Exchange It.	15
STEP 7:	Arrange It.	17
STEP 8:	Attain It.	19
STEP 9:	Manage It.	21
STEP 10:	Mind It.	23
	Conclusion	25

DARE 2 D.R.E.A.M.

ACKNOWLEDGMENTS

I'd like to acknowledge my family, who have always been there for me with voluntary and involuntary support... I'd like to thank all of my friends for a continuous understanding of 'My Next Great Idea'. And lastly, I appreciate all of my mentors for talking me off the ledge when I needed it and at times pushing me over it because I wouldn't have gone otherwise...

Thank You for the D.R.E.A.M.:

AT&T · Arrow Records · Best Buy
The Coca-Cola Company
Electrolux · Emory University
LG Electronics · Lowe's · NASCAR
Neiman Marcus · Room & Board · SmartWater

.

DARE 2 D.R.E.A.M.

INTRODUCTION
Let's Get It Started…

For the longest time I just wanted to create something... Something that mattered... Something that would help people... Something that would inspire them and push them forward to achieve the next level of their success, whatever that looked like, and not take 17 hours of their life reading a book to do it...

Dare 2 D.R.E.A.M. is just that... a quick-reference, pocket guide that gets to the point of how to take a step-by-step approach to the basics of building a brand successfully. It is not some puffed up and empty thought piece, but rather 10 universal truths that apply to all of us in some form or fashion for our everyday lives. I had this concept to do a 'Dr. Seuss meets Business' book for quite some time and what's funny, is that when I looked at the title/subtitle combination it just spoke to me. I laugh because the latter part says 'whether it be a person, product, or project...' and it's so true because the information housed within applies to any situation whether you're creating the life you imagined or building a brand that's an extension of it. Many people ask, "Tony, have you really used these steps to build brands?!?" And emphatically, I answer and say yes. This very book is a result that. Now... has it been exactly as I imagined the entire time?!? Absolutely not! I was still in the process of learning how to make it all happen, but what I realized as I finished one project and moved on to the next, it was the same 10 steps repeated over and over again to help me achieve what I was trying to do. To give you better insight, my favorite movie of all time is Hitch starring Will Smith. What he did for men and women, I do for businesses and brands. He was a dating consultant... I'm a branding consultant. And here is how it all relates... The best thing about being a consultant is that before a client comes along, the consultant has already gotten it wrong. So the client is the recipient of information that has already been through the process of failure and that has now been adjusted and presented with proven success.

You know it's kinda cool... what took me so long to write this book is that I didn't think I was the proper spokesperson for it. I told myself that no one wanted to hear from me and that I needed to achieve more success, get more fame and notoriety, etc. But what was so crazy is that I would always have people asking me how I did XYZ. This came from job recruiters when I would interview for consultant positions, friends, family, other entrepreneurs, etc. For the last few years since our win for Best Social Event at The 2011 Allie Awards for an internationally recognized project I created called The Atlanta Food Rave®, I have become the go-to-guy for branding and brand strategy. I have been invited by top-tier business schools to assess the case studies of their Sr. MBA candidates, featured on The Wall Street Business Network and even highlighted in articles and editorials, but for some reason I just didn't buy into the fact that I was actually qualified to write about what I knew or a better way to put it... 'What I failed through.' My background includes over 10 years of experience in marketing and branding and I have even worked with companies such as Neiman Marcus, Coca-Cola and SmartWater, but I still didn't think I knew and/or did enough... And it is in this point right here wherein the entire key to bringing *Dare 2 D.R.E.A.M.* comes alive... You have to start! If you never start you can never finish. So many people fail in life because of a simple lack of execution. Not saying that their idea was bad or anything like that... They just never believed in themselves enough or in some cases were just too lazy to start. And with this, you get where this entire book is taking you... I only know the path because I have traveled it, but there is nothing that I nor anyone else can do to help you if you don't start.

With that said... This book is meant to be an ongoing, interactive experience of branding. You may be on some steps for a month... some even longer, and that's okay... What we all have to realize is that we haven't lost until we quit. *Dare 2 D.R.E.A.M.* is a conversation between friends. And because you are my friend... I'm more than happy to share my thoughts and experience with you. Branding is simple... People make it complicated.

STEP 1:
DEFINE IT.

What is it?!?

"If you don't know where you are going…
Any road will get you there."
- The Cheshire Cat from Alice in Wonderland

A great idea is a wonderful thing to have, but if you don't spend the time to actually whittle down this mass of cognitive marble, you will never get to a point to where you can share it with the world. Many times we walk around with these delusions of grandeur that happen in our minds, but we never fully figure out what it is or what to call it or even what it really looks like. A simple task that you can do to help you define your dream, vision, plan or goal is to define it by five points. The brand of Tony Rouse is defined and described by:

(1.) Creative (2.) Energetic (3.) Bold
(4.) Custom (5.) Defined.

In everything I go to do, these five things resonate throughout. To say this is an easy task would be a bold-faced lie. You are going to have to spend time with yourself and/or your project and get away to a space to be alone with your thoughts and come up with the things that define and represent who you are and what you're trying to do. Here's the biggest kicker of 'The Defining Moment': If you don't know what it is, who you are and/or what you do… neither will we. See the end from the beginning and work backwards to help establish brand identity.

STEP 2: DESIGN IT.

Let Me "See"…

"Design is a funny word.
Some people think design means how it looks.
But of course, if you dig deeper, it's really how it works."
- Steve Jobs

Design is not just limited to the fonts and colors of packaging. Design in essence, is functionality. I am one of those people that when I am creating something, I have to break it before somebody buys it. *Meaning:* I am going to take my idea, my dream, my plan, my goal, my vision and 'poke as many holes in it' as I can so that when it's designed, it's fully functional in all that it's been called to do.

As a creator, you should know every twist and turn as it relates to your product before anyone else gets a chance to play with it. Personally, I have pages and pages of notes from a dream journal that I call 'The Life of Tony Rouse' and over the years I have written down many ideas that I could define, but couldn't design. After a while, I would put the projects aside and come back later to possibly re-imagine and re-work them, but I knew that the design and functionality piece had to work first or I was simply stuck in this phase of the project.

There is something to be said about good design, but there is something that can be felt by great design. In all that we go to do… we must be great. The key to effective branding is keeping it simple.

STEP 3: REHEARSE IT.

If you don't practice to perfection, why should anyone else care?

"The Relentless Pursuit of Perfection."
- Lexus

Too many people in this day and age are amateurs posing as experts. It saddens me to think that so many people are duped by individuals that have no proven track record of success, but yet and still are celebrated for non-existent accomplishments. I will say that at some point everyone has to start, but for clarity... be a lifelong student. Teach what you've been taught, but let the experiences that other people have shared with you define you as an expert. Taking on a title that hasn't been given is the quickest way to lose something that you never had.

As it relates to preparation, get to the point to where you go over your materials and have them ready behind the scenes before you invite the public to be witness to something you have set for grand display. You should've spent so much time with yourself that your project, product or plan is second nature to you and that it is literally a part of the fabric of your very being. This is also another time to where you can find bits and pieces that you might've missed in the design phase so that you will be able to make the proper correction. Never be an individual that is willing to present without practice. You're not going to be perfect and that's okay. You have started. We are going to finish and will execute excellence in every step of the way.

STEP 4: REWIND IT.

Practice Makes Permanent…

"First of all, what happens is, when you're good at something, you spend a lot of time with it. People identify you with that sport, so it becomes part of your identity."
- Mike "Coach K" Krzyzewski

When I was working in the music industry and a part of an organization with international reach to 6 countries and 23 territories in the US, one of the things that I innately understood was that just because something would work a certain way in Atlanta, it might not be true for a setup in Australia. Thankfully, we had an amazing global team that could assist with the translation of culture to make all of our jobs easier, but on our end in the States, we still had to know what we were doing and/or talking about before anything could even attempt to be translated.

The phase of 'Rewind It.' is simply the art of rehearsing the situation over and over and over and over again until we can't get it wrong. We are going for mastery. Now this doesn't mean that we are not in the process of prototypes and testing, but rather this is how we, as I mentioned earlier, break a brand. As it relates to what is being shaped and formed, we must remember that practice makes permanent and how we approach something in our 'off-time' says a lot about what we do in our 'on-time'. This step won't take forever, but is necessary.

STEP 5:
EMBRACE IT.
This is your dream…

*"There is no passion to be found playing small –
in settling for a life that is less than the one
you are capable of living."*
- Nelson Mandela

There is a distinct difference between management and ownership. When you manage something… you take care of it and then return it. But when you own something… it is a part of you and there is just a certain way that you treat something because you are the person that is ultimately responsible for it. A great example is a babysitter versus a parent. A babysitter will look after someone's child for a very short period of time, but a parent must oversee that child's journey into adulthood because everything concerning that child is their responsibility. So to embrace your dream, plan, vision or goal really means to have it become the embodiment of who you are every day.

If we are speaking in terms of a product… this is fulfilled with a guarantee, tagline or slogan. As mentioned in the 'Define It.' stage, when people attend anything that is created or produced by Tony Rouse, there are five elements that will always be present. For me it is an inherent guarantee that I am going to deliver on these very things. Your 'brand' has to mimic and match your message. Far too often customers and clients are let down because they had hope in a product that only had hype.

STEP 6: EXCHANGE IT.

If no one knows about your dream, how will it ever impact and help others?

"Tell me and I forget.
Teach me and I remember.
Involve me and I learn."
- Benjamin Franklin

A brand is simply doing what you said you were going to do each and every time a customer interacts with you. Many people know that the most effective form of marketing and advertising is word-of-mouth. The only difference is that today our medium of messages are no longer just our immediate physical circles, but rather we are all on worldwide platforms that now include the likes of Instagram, Facebook, SnapChat, Twitter, etc. Ideas have to have the opportunity to spread, but you also have to be well versed in what you do so that when you tell people… they can tell people, that tell people… about who you are and what you do.

As previously mentioned, the first run won't be perfect, but do your absolute best to create and start with what you do know. Build up a community by starting with close friends and family that know you best, then work towards outer layers as this movement all begins to take shape. From a digital integration aspect, factor in the use of a hashtag so people can stay up with you and what you're doing. For our announcements, encouragement and quotes my team uses: #MeetTonyRouse. *Your Job:* 'Make it easy so the world can make it known.'

STEP 7:
ARRANGE IT.
Set Yourself Up for Success.

"For a business to survive and thrive, 100 percent of all the systems must be functioning and accountable."
- Robert T. Kiyosaki

It's all about the system. A system has to be in place for the product and/or project to be able to have what we will refer to as a flow. If you imagine a river, it will flow as long as there's no dam blocking it, but the moment a dam comes in place... you have now held up the process of the water from reaching its intended destination. The same situation applies when you relate that to people and your product... With a blockage, you have people suffering because they can't get access to what you have to offer. So you must arrange a flow for things to happen for you and also support the system you have built.

Earlier we discussed a brand is simply doing what you said you'd do and the best example of that is a visual representation I call, *'Marketing Mathematics'*:

MARKETING MATHEMATICS:

$$brand = \left(\frac{trust}{perception + experience}\right)^{*[time]}$$

This formula will help you understand how to build a strong brand for life. *Explanation:* A brand is built by the trust established from public perception & experience over the course of time.

STEP 8: ATTAIN IT.

Fight… and Go Get It.

"You're the best around...
Nothing's gonna ever keep you down."
- Theme Song from The Karate Kid

Many times this process is not going to be one that is a walk in the park. You will literally have to fight for everything that you have and let me say this again… that's okay. What we must understand is that this fight is not necessarily going to come from developing quick and strong hands, but rather it is going to involve a mental mindset of toughness where you have to believe that you not only have something that people need, but most importantly… something that they want, want to be a part of and can't live without.

The real fight that we are talking about takes place between your ears and behind your eyes. It is a fight in your mind. You are going to want to quit. You are going to want to walk away. You are going to want to throw your hands up and decide that this is not for you and then question why you even decided to pursue this process in the first place. But then all of a sudden… you'll have a glimmer of light that will fill you with hope to keep pressing on. Because here's the reality…What you think about is what you think about. If we can get to the point to where we can think the thoughts that will help us be effective and block out the ones that are detrimental, we can win and claim victory every time.

STEP 9: MANAGE IT.

You are in Charge…

*"Learn to say 'No' to the good
so you can say 'Yes' to the best."*
- John C. Maxwell

So many times we let our projects and products consume us while we don't pay them the real attention that they so desperately need. From a management perspective, we have to remember that we still have to cross the finish line with a completed product. Many times people get stuck in the 'Rehearse It.' and 'Rewind It.' phases and forget... that was only steps 3 and 4 out of 10. Finish the project and manage accordingly so we can set our next vision which of course begins at step 1.

What is critical and crucial about 'Manage It.' is that we have to be responsible for our priorities and make sure that our entire project set up is accurate. We have to be mindful of our intended destination. Always remember to see the end from the beginning. Far too often we lose sight of why we got started on something in the first place and when we get away from the vision, we then realize we've moved away from what we initially designed. We end up lost because now we don't have a foundation or blueprint to build from or return to.

STEP 10: MIND IT.

Your Dream should always be Front and Center…

"If you wanna be somebody…
If you wanna go somewhere…
You better wake up and pay attention."
- Sister Act 2: Back in the Habit

As we mentioned earlier, we think about what we think about. From the deep recesses of our mind… we started with an idea that we then introduced to the public and then created a platform (in some cases) for something that never existed before. We brought it to fruition and now are able to enjoy the fruits of our labor… Right?!? Well this is actually a loaded question. Can you enjoy what you've produced?!? Yes. But should you revel in it?!? No. In other words, don't get to the point where we have done all of this hard work and then don't 'Mind the things we Mined.'

When I think about success as it relates to products and product production, I've learned that there is no final destination. We are in a constant state of learning and what we are able to gather when we 'Mind It.' is that we are able to replay the victories that helped us reach this point. We realize the areas of development where we spent too much time and we can record overall results for a better output on the next endeavor. Realize this… Your job is never done because without paying attention to the areas that need updates and upkeep, you can easily find your person, product and/or project obsolete.

CONCLUSION:
Let's Bring It All Together…

"If you can dream it, you can do it."
- Walt Disney

The best way I can sum up this entire conversation and the need for all of us to look forward and *Dare 2 D.R.E.A.M.* is via something I wrote some time ago entitled *'The Beauty of Regret':*

The Beauty of Regret

The beauty of regret is that there is no beauty at all.
Looking back on 'shouldas', 'couldas' and 'wouldas'
is nothing but a wall…
We move to make them fall,
but nothing happens at all.

We cannot focus on what is in the rearview mirror,
but instead on that which is coming into picture clearer.

Every day I wake, looking forward to new horizons
Excited by the opportunities to seize
vast oceanic landscapes like Poseidon.

At this point I won't regret the things I didn't do,
but I will go after those things yet to be accomplished
until I'm through.

So know this…
no one can stop me from whatever I'm going to get
because all that I am is all that I'm meant.

- Always Dare 2 D.R.E.A.M. -

* **<u>A Special Note:</u>** If you have found this book to be informative, enlightening, humorous & engaging... Let me know! My various contact information has been provided in the 'About the Author' section and I look forward to learn of your experience. Also, please share your recommendation of this title with your colleagues, friends and social networks.

Thank You.
-Tony Rouse

Fun Fact: Did you notice that there is no printed text on the back cover of this book?!? I was inspired by billionaire hotelier, Steve Wynn, who when he created his namesake hotel Wynn Las Vegas, chose not put the 'show' on the outside of the venue like in his previous hotel ventures Bellagio and Treasure Island. So the reason this 'book has no back' is because I decided to house the information and adventure inside as opposed to presenting a full display merely for people passing by. In other words... Thank you for reading.

ABOUT THE AUTHOR

Tony Rouse is a Brand Strategy Specialist known as The Curator of High-End Experiences whose revolutionary concepts and projects have achieved international exposure and acclaim. He is a Myers-Briggs hybrid of "The Executive" (ENTJ) and "The Giver" (ENFJ) who created and defined the term, Fully Integrated Lifestyle Marketing (F.I.L.M.) which, as he sees it, takes an unconventional approach to traditional advertising by seamlessly creating experiences for brands in the lives of their target consumers and as such, has become the signature of his award-winning style. Having worked with over 25 Fortune 500 companies in the varied capacities of advisement, representation and consultation, he has also been an emcee on national tours for both NASCAR and Universal Records. By the age of 18, he was a featured performer at Carnegie Hall and today serves as a guest contributor for The Wall Street Business Network. Coupled with a healthy dose of witty wisdom and humorous understanding of the rapidly changing state of consumer affairs, taste, preferences and selection, he effortlessly relates to a world inundated with ever-evolving technology.

For More Information: www.MeetTonyRouse.com
Facebook/Instagram/Twitter: @MeetTonyRouse
Email: SayHello@MeetTonyRouse.com

Additional Titles by Tony Rouse:

My Life as a Thought…
A Journey of Grace, Growth & God

Presentation Pep Talk:
The 20-Minute Quick Fix

Takeover Tuesday:
55 Short Stories to Help You
Win in Business & Life

www.ingramcontent.com/pod-product-compliance
Lightning Source LLC
Chambersburg PA
CBHW070948210326
41520CB00021B/7111